PRESCHOOL READING SUCCESS
IN JUST
FIVE MINUTES A DAY

THE FUN & SIMPLE WAY
FOR EFFECTIVE READING

By
LOUISE V. MOORE

WHAT PEOPLE ARE SAYING ABOUT

PRESCHOOL READING SUCCESS

IN JUST

FIVE MINUTES A DAY

"For anyone who is trying to teach their toddler to read and set them above the average, I would recommend Preschool Reading Success in Just Five Minutes a Day."

~ **Angela Pettus,** Elementary Teacher

"Preschool Reading Success in Just Five Minutes a Day taps into the most essential component of reading. This book typifies why Louise Moore has proven herself to be one of the emerging voices in children literacy for 2015 and beyond. Preschool Reading Success in Just Five Minutes a Day is refreshing, concise and brimming over with practical wisdom."

~ **Eric Andrews,** Business Department Chair

"I started using Louise's methods to teach my daughter to read at age 3. I was a bit skeptical at first and didn't want to push my daughter, but she absolutely loves our daily reading time!"

~ **Darla Bittner,** Mother

CONTENTS

SPECIAL GIFT FOR READERS

Get more valuable reading resources for you and your child or grandchildren by visiting our website: www.childrensreadingsuccess.com

INTRODUCTION

Before age 3, our children were reading short words on billboards, signs, and on passing trucks. They had not memorized them from TV ads as their grandmother had surmised. They were reading on their own. One day my mother who had been a school teacher, and was caring for my 3 year old son could not wait to come home to tell me that he was reading signs. The words that he read were only three letters long, but it was definitely a great start. She said "I was so excited that I almost drove off the road." Several years later, my son's kindergarten teacher commented to me, "You do realize that your son knows how to read." Yes, of course I knew. I taught him by using the simple methods described in this delightful little book. It is so much fun, and I know that you too will discover this same rewarding result.

My son was tested for reading just as he turned 5 years old with kindergarten 6 months away, and he was almost at the third grade level. I had the same success with my daughter, and her teacher had the same glowing remarks about her reading ability. Yes, of course, I knew that they could read many words by kindergarten as they understood basic phonetic sounds.

Because of this ability, their elementary school teachers judged them to be very bright, and my children lived up to this wonderful expectation. They felt great about school, and about themselves. This one ability paved the way to enormous success all through their schooling.

Their elementary school principal was astonished when I said that I had easily taught them to read at home. It is not hard. It is simply learning the basic "noises" that each letter contains in silly, happy, energetic and fun words, and then combining/blending these noises into words. My children never remembered learning how to read because it was as natural and effortless as breathing and sleeping, and it only took 5 minutes or less a day. Yes, there is 5 minute a day parent involvement, but you have to talk to them about something other than disciplining them. And this happy talk creates a joyful connection between the two of you.

When my children were preschoolers and now with my grandchildren, this learning routine was an integral part of our everyday lives, and I know you will experience our same happy result.

Now in 2015, I am observing that schools require a child to be quite proficient in reading by the first grade, and this can be overwhelming. I recently heard this anxiety from a mother who was well aware of this, and didn't know what to do. Of course I told her about my ideas, and she couldn't wait to hear them.

My granddaughter was just tested in the first grade, and the results are that she is reading 125 words per minute with 100% comprehension, and is the best reader in her class. We were thrilled, and the method described in these pages is the reason. She is 6 years old and has been reading for several years. My four year old grandson is also well on his way to becoming a good and happy reader too, and will easily move into kindergarten and the first grade with this ability.

Boys who tend to mature later will definitely be helped by having this skill naturally taught to them. If you have their reading well on its way during their early years, their attitude to their future schooling will be a wonderful experience for them as they have passed this first very big and significant hurdle in their education. If not, their sense of accomplishment and confidence will suffer, and their joy and enthusiasm for going to school will diminish.

If children have difficulty learning to read in a school environment for whatever reasons, they can believe that they are not good enough or smart enough or that something is wrong with them on a conscious or subconscious level. Let's erase any chance of that. For them to think later that they need to catch up if they have trouble with reading isn't a solid or confident place to begin their education. I want them to feel early success in reading which I am hoping will spill over into their other subjects and into other areas of their lives.

In fact, reinforcing a child's view of himself in this context of success in reading can instill in them that they are wonderful, smart, loved and more than good enough to keep learning and doing the right thing in life. Success is a wonderful and motivating feeling. It was my observation, that dropping out of school for any child who has been a strong early reader with many interests is less likely to drop out of school in high school. This timeless learning ability can be easily taught, and be the catalyst for developing and supporting the whole child in a very loving and stress free manner. Both of you will love this process!

Less than one third of elementary students are proficient in reading by the end of the third grade. Forty percent of all high school graduates are functionally illiterate. I just read that only 7% of eighth graders in Detroit can read proficiently. A piece of research published in Developmental Psychology in 1997 showed first grade reading ability was closely linked to 11th grade academic achievement (WSJ 9-16-14.) Statistics like this are in the news all of the time.

A child's educational future in all areas of study depends on his ability to read, and it is our absolute responsibility as parents to be certain that our children can and will read using these easy and playful methods. Allow me to teach YOU (parents and grandparents) to teach your child to read at home. It will only take five minutes a day which will be the most important FIVE minutes you can spend with them at this stage of their lives. .

READING CHALLENGES TO OVERCOME

For many children, learning to read in a school environment can be daunting, and maybe even impossible. There are many diversions, distractions, and obstacles in a classroom and many programs simply do not connect with your child. This was my experience as a child even though I was labeled as gifted. The home is a child's first classroom, and parents are their first teachers. Home is the best place to start. A loving and attentive parent or caregiver can happily incorporate my ideas in laying the groundwork for a successful reading future. Reading is the number one challenge of a child in the early years of his schooling, so give him this real head-start to his future education.

Do not forfeit the education of your child solely to the schools, TV, cable, computer programs, video games, DVDs, the general culture, or any of the rest of present day media/high tech diversions. Our society and culture inundate and distract our children with stimulation of all sorts: far more than any other society in the history of the world. So you have to get in there with your child with this fun work as early as possible.

The power of parenting determines a child's future...her self-confidence, her curiosity, her verbal ability, her intelligence, her loving emotional health, and certainly her educational future. The attentive mother or caregiver changes everything for the good as she teaches these reading skills; speaking and reading to her and actively showing her love and affection within the pages of Dr. Seuss or the thousands of childrens' books that are available now in so many formats. The future of our country depends on MOTHERS.....WOW!!!

And as far as the pop culture invading your home, I heard a speaker once say, "Don't allow an alien culture to come into your home with TV on 24/7, along with music and videos that do not promote your view on life." It is so easy and enticing to have the TV used as a baby sitter, and sometimes in the early morning and late afternoon before dinner this is all right, but please do not let this take over their lives. Look at the culture in your own home. With what do you surround your child? Do you have bookshelves full of wonderful books? Do they see you reading which is, by the way, a great stress reliever? What is the art on the walls, what movies do you watch, and what music flows through your house? Are you respectful of each other? Do love and respect dominate your household? The culture in your home is of paramount importance to your child's development and their attitude to learning. Understanding the written word will help them escape the popular culture (of TV, movies, high tech diversions, and popular music) so that they become more thoughtful and insightful as they discover their own true God given talents. Then their authentic, free, and successful lives will emerge. Learning to read early can change their entire lives. I truly believe this, and I sincerely want the children in your home to learn to read. Let them learn to read now so that they can read to learn later.

THEIR VERY EARLY LEARNING YEARS

Children are naturally curious and are receptive, and will easily take to early reading, especially and very importantly if there is an element of fun in the process. They will love the attention that they will receive from you, and you will love this new connection with your child that this learning opportunity creates. This visionary program will become the new communication between you two. There is a wonderful window between the ages of 3 and 5 yrs. old when you can have their full attention before they are more physically active and want to run outside to play. This delightful little book addresses this time.

FROM BIRTH TO 3

Firstly, all parents and caregivers must realize that a child needs to hear many words lovingly directed at him or her from birth on, even though at first he will not understand them. Speaking to a baby and happily acknowledging his existence in a very warm, gentle, and loving way needs to be established from the very beginning. This is the foundation for future reading. How? They need to hear happy and loving positive conversation directed to them so that they hear many words that will become familiar to them. Sadly, many small children are ignored, tolerated or simply left alone. We cannot do that. Show your child the natural world as you would imagine indigenous people would show the living world to their offspring. Before 1 year old, show her, touch it, name it, let her point to it as you name and admire the trees, bushes, bugs, flowers, the sky, airplanes, birds, ants, dogs etc. Be excited and involved in the moment. No, you don't have to do this every moment. But show her your own enthusiasm as you rediscover life through her eyes. Having her point seems to focus her attention." Do you see that bird? What is he doing? Is he flying high in the blue sky, or sitting in the tree? Where is his nest? It is probably in the tree over there. I wonder where his children are. If you can manage to have a bird feeder with bird seed from the supermarket within easy view, this is a fabulous thing for a very young child to watch. This idea brings great excitement. What else can you both focus on as you encourage emotional and verbal interaction? "Look at the beautiful flowers." Go from house to house as you walk along or push them in a stroller, and point these out. Don't bring your babe into an outdoor environment without commenting on what is going on in it. Verbalize what you see. "Where's the dog? Do you hear it barking? What color is he? Is he white, brown, or black? Look at the children over there. What are they doing? Let us go to the park. Do you want to go on the swings, the monkey bars or the slide? Look at the airplane high up in the sky. I wonder where they are going" Do you see that speech directed to them is the basis of reading? A child slowly becomes comfortable with language and familiar with many words through much loving repetition, and puts together these outdoor experiences (birds, flowers, dogs, airplanes etc.) with the pictures in the books, magazines and on cereal boxes that they have at home (which you will point out.) All of this is a fun and very rewarding way to be with your child at this early stage of his educational development.

Babies and very young children are little trusting sponges who absorb far more than parents or caregivers realize. Recent studies have confirmed that a parent's poor use of vocabulary through the first 36 months of a child's life can have a dramatic and negative impact on a child's intellectual future. Children who have limited exposure to the spoken word have greater difficulty in learning to read. Small children need far more than custodial care with the TV on all day. They need love most of all, attention, validation, acknowledgment and respect. Listen to them as though they matter. Take their comments seriously. It is said that if a mother is trapped in poverty or is overwhelmed by financial and emotional stress, that she is less likely to speak to her very young children in a positive manner. Understandably as parents, we can all relate to that, but perhaps consciously recognizing this point will be helpful to parents or caregivers as they view the importance of speaking and reading out loud to their children.

Recently my adult daughter's friend was at our house with her 8 mo. old son. I spoke directly to Eric for a few moments. He was completely in the moment and stared at me as I spoke to him in a quietly animated manner. I told him "that Thanksgiving was coming and wait until you wrap your gums around some pumpkin pie... oh boy...And I imagine that your Grandmother makes wonderful stuffing and mashed potatoes with gravy.... oh yes, yes, and just wait until you taste cranberries with the turkey...ooh yum... And Christmas comes after Thanksgiving with Santa Claus, presents and a Christmas tree. You will love this etc. etc." He was transfixed as I held him, and spoke directly to him. I spoke to him as though I expected him to say something back, and it seemed as though he wished that he could. This is the type of chatter I am discussing. No, he didn't know what I was saying, but he was witnessing language, and there was something very positive going on with his cognitive skills. Everyone in the room could see it. On the way home from our house and since then, his Mother, said that he is babbling more. Yes, he is imitating language in his beginning ways, and this is his foundation for reading. A Mother's, Father's or caretaker's familiarity with speech and verbal response is very important. Please keep the chatter going in a positive, happy, and loving manner.

READING TO YOUR CHILDREN

Read out loud to your children. I remember Tom Selleck reading a sports article to the baby in the movie, "Three Men and A Baby." He had just the right tone in his voice and the right body language as he directed his eyes to the baby's eyes while reading to her. You know that you are connecting when the baby watches you intently. New pathways to the brain are being developed and their cognitive abilities are growing. Research has proven that a child's first years are critical to language development. Never speak down to children in words or in attitude even as babies. This is so important. Respect their intellectual growth and awareness as you surround them with many loving words. Watch as they listen with their bright eyes and be amazed with your facial expressions as they grasp the means of communication.

Children love to have their own books, and to be able to read by themselves. Reading will connect them to experiences beyond their own lives, and will create the future direction for their schooling years. When you go to the library for baby and toddler books, maybe you could pick up a book for yourself. Let them watch you as you model reading to them. They will understand by your example that reading a newspaper, magazine or book is an activity of great value. And now of course there are KINDLES for children, but holding a real book is the best.

WHEN TO START

Start teaching them the names of the letters around 2 years old. Sing the ABC song to them. NAMING the letters is altogether different than the sounds that they make. This comes later. There are letter stickers that make this fun, and you can draw them on paper or a blackboard. As you draw a D for example say, here is a stick with a big bump also say let's color this D together. Each letter that I describe will be explained in a toddler friendly way. They will remember these letters. All of this is interactive and not just plugging your babe into a DVD or a TV show.

Literacy is now seen as a civil right, but working with language and reading in the home is a parent's responsibility. Much is at stake with a child's education, and no government or school program can have as much influence as the parent, grandparent or caregiver teaching them. We are responsible for our children's' future, and early vocabulary and reading skills are profound in their ramifications. The early ability to read will give them an enormous sense of self-esteem and confidence as they excel in kindergarten, as well as the first and second grades and beyond. School will become fun, and they will look forward to going as they are already familiar and successful with this first big hurdle. A child needs to be positively clicked into a happy way of living and behaving, and by using some of these following happy and energetic words and phrases, this wonderful attitude along with reading skills will be achieved. These early years are the perfect time to introduce reading into their lives. They want to be around you, and they want your attention. In a few years, they will want to be outside and running. Now is the perfect time.

Our children are being exposed to a profound change in access to information both good and bad. They must be taught to use the internet to a positive result. For older children reading books for fun is changing to reading on the internet. Cultural changes are shifting now, but the fun, comfort and love of snuggling up with a good book with your toddler will never change.

GETTING STARTED

The first steps are visual and interactive. By this, I mean that you will draw each capital and lower case letter one at a time in a very appealing and child friendly manner that I will describe. Your child will watch as you carefully draw and name each letter.

The second step is verbal. As you name each letter, have her repeat the name of the letter back to you. Then you will sound out the "noise" that each letter makes. You will catch on to these steps quickly. I will give you the basic sounds as well as the word examples that will illustrate each "noise." Make sure again that she repeats the name of the letter and the "noise" each letter makes, back to you. There will be a lot of back and forth conversation and responses. I need to emphasize again that the NAME of a letter is altogether different from the NOISE that each letter makes. You must make this very clear to her. Have her repeat both the name and the "noise" a letter makes until she is very confident in doing so. Take your time as there is no hurry. Also have her repeat back some of the words that demonstrate the initial sounds that you are teaching: the more fun and sillier the word the better. TAKE NOTE OF THE WORDS THAT SHE THINKS ARE PARTICULARLY FUNNY, SILLY OR HAS SOME MEANINGFUL CONNECTION WITH HER LIFE. I have many words from which to choose. Repeat these often as you emphasize their sound. This is very important as she will be more likely to remember the sound you are teaching when it is associated with something that gets her attention, and which her makes her laugh and be happy. When she repeats back the correct sound and the corresponding words, you must engage her with many hugs, kisses, smiles, laughter, and true admiration. Bring her stuffed animal into these activities that will smother her in kisses as you press its furry face into her neck and cheeks. It is PARTY TIME when correct responses are given!! The expectation that if she correctly repeats the sound back to you, she will have a fabulous, fun, and very motivating pay-off is a great incentive for wanting more. Start using some of the fun examples that I have included. Excitement starts for both of you as you say and demonstrate each initial sound using the fun, silly and familiar examples for each letter that I will provide in the following pages. Come on now...this isn't work...FIVE minutes a day is all that you will need.

AND AWAY WE GO

With a child as young as 2 ½ to 3 years old just dive in. The best way to set up is with a large bean bag placed in front of a chalk board. Or alternatively have pillows piled up on the floor in front of a chalk board. Or simply have both of you sit on the couch with a notebook size piece of paper or colored paper would be nice in order to grab their attention...whatever is convenient and realistic for you. The manner that you use isn't as important as the fun, good humor and enthusiasm that you will bring to all of this.

Draw and name one letter at a time until she thoroughly understands it. Slowly and very carefully draw the capital letter and then the lower case letter. Call the capital letter the big Daddy letter, and the lower case the little boy/girl letter. Let her color the letter that you have drawn.

Be very casual with absolutely no pressure in your voice or manner. I will provide a few silly comments and you will think of some on your own. They will be intent on what you are doing if you make it fun for them. Use several words and phrases from the samples of child friendly words and phrases that I will give you including words for animals, food, colors, funny names, and a wide variety of other words. Please choose words that you are certain that your child recognizes as well as a few that she doesn't know so as to enlarge her vocabulary. Use especially funny and familiar words to her. This silliness holds their attention. Yes, we know that their attention span is short, so catch their attention with fun words including family names, names of animals stuffed and real, and names of dolls, favorite foods and toys. You will notice that there is a zone...a place that captures their attention. Find it.

After you have taught one or two letters or more a week, go about your day leaving the chalkboard or paper behind. Start on-going happy and upbeat chatter using the words in these pages while emphasizing the sounds/noises. Glance at these pages for inspiration. Sometimes it is hard to think of the appropriate words for each letter that your child will understand, so I have included many examples. The best words are the fun words that will make them laugh, be alert and create an energy that will inspire them to want more. Find this happy and energetic groove. Keep having him repeat back to you the sound you are learning at the moment.

You will be introducing a few words to him that he doesn't know. Tell them the meaning. This is wonderful as he is expanding his vocabulary. Look at pictures in books every day. Comment on the pictures with words that start with the sounds he is learning. A child needs to know what a penguin is before he could possibly know how to read the word, penguin. Cereal boxes are a great place to look at letters and silly words.

Children are very curious, receptive and love to learn. In this process of language and reading development, a new joy and bonding will happen between you two. This is one of the side benefits you will experience as you more deeply connect with your daughter or son. As you go through the letters in the following pages, she will learn to read slowly, naturally and easily, and with NO stress or pushing. The approach that I am advocating is one of relaxation and fun with much repetition. I taught my children in this vein, and then let them play and enjoy being children. They moved into elementary school work very easily and successfully with a great background in reading comprehension, and this program greatly enlarged their vision of life. They loved school because they had such early successes in reading, and their teachers were absolutely amazed with them. I never told the teachers that I had easily taught them to read at home. I let them believe that my guys were just smart, and that they were excellent teachers. I later sometimes wondered if the teachers treated them differently because they were so successfully responsive with this first challenge of reading. Maybe they thought that they were such good teachers that this must be the outcome of their marvelous efforts, but it created a self-fulfilling prophesy for their educational future. In any event, our children had nothing but great success in the early grades of elementary school, and throughout all of their education. I believe that this reading program formed a great foundation for all of their schooling years yet to come, and did wonders for their attitudes about school. They were winners before they even set foot in the classroom.

NOW LET'S GET STARTED WITH EACH LETTER...JUMP IN ...LET'S GO

A as in ANT

DRAW a capital A saying here is a stick that goes this way / and another stick that goes this other way \ with a monkey bar in-between. Say that the name of this letter is A, and then write a lowercase saying that this is a little circle with a tail. Tell her that there is a big daddy "A" and a little kid "a."

Always describe the drawing of letters in a toddler- friendly way. Then tell her that the letter A has a sound or better yet, say that it makes a "NOISE." Tell her that there is a big difference between the name of the letter and the noise that the letter makes.

The noise of the letter A is "ah" as in ANT. Let her repeat the sound several times ah ah ah....EXCELLENT! I think that you can hear it ...very good ....one more time say ah ahah. Have her repeat it. Have her understand it well enough to move on to a few words that you know will make her smile, and catch her attention. Remember to only take FIVE minutes.

SAY. Let me see, what words start with the AH/AH sound? AMAZING, let's dance AROUND AND AROUND. You are ABSOLUTELY AMAZING. We need to hug AGAIN AND AGAIN. We need AN ADVENTURE today with some ACTION AND ACTIVITY! AH AH...can you hear the sound...AWESOME (hugs and kisses now with lots of happiness)

Remind her, can you hear the sound A..ah ah sound? Say, "You are so smart." Compliment her in a big way when she repeats the sound or repeats an A word with a big kiss from the teddy bear or tickle them with much happiness and smiles...Make them feel as if the circus is in town with much happy attention. No tickles if they cannot think of the sound. Let them roll around on the floor on the pillows and enjoy themselves a lot. They will be very enthusiastic if this is their payoff.

Pick and choose which words and phrases will connect with your babe.

Is the kitty ASLEEP. Do you think that your teddy bear is ASLEEP too? Have you seen the little ANTS outside? They are not ASLEEP. They are running AROUND. Can you hear ANY ANIMALS in the neighborhood? Let's see what other words start with the AH noise? ACHOO. I sneezed. Excuse me. Let us go ACROSS the yard to ASK our neighbor, Mrs. ANDERSON if she would like some ANIMAL crackers or some APPLES. We are AT home, but your brother/sister is AT school. The little fish live in the AQUARIUM. We are learning the ALPHABET. Do you hear the AH sound? I AGREE, ANYONE hungry for APPLESAUCE? I AM. Can you repeat the A sound back to me ALOUD? AWESOME! AMAZING! I have to ANSWER the phone. What is this ALL ABOUT? ALL ABOARD says the train conductor. I think that you deserve an AWARD today for being AN excellent girl. I am ASTONISHED! ANNABELLE AND ANDREW ARE ADULTS. Let's play AROUND this AFTERNOON, ALL RIGHT? What is your ANSWER, my ADORABLE child? I AGREE, I APPROVE, ALL right. Do you hear the AH sound/noise in ALL of this? Do we need AN ADVENTURE AT the AMUSEMENT Park? I want to ASK you. Do you have AN APPETITE for ALPHABET soup? ANYONE hungry? Sounds APPETIZING to me. This ADVENTURE book is ABOUT some ASTRONAUTS. There are too many ADS on TV. ATTENTION please, I want to ASK you a question. What is your ADDRESS? No ANSWER...hmmmm.... let us go outside to look at the numbers on the mailbox. So ANYWAY, ARE you AWAKE or ARE you ASLEEP? Is ANYBODY there? ABOVE ALL, I will ALWAYS love you.

Other A words that can be worked into the conversation. AH AH....Hold onto my hand so that we can go ACROSS the street, We are ALIVE! ALOHA, ANCHOR on a ship, I APPLAUD you, AMIGO, ADD this to our list. Where is your ANKLE, I ADORE you is ANOTHER way of saying that I love you, let me ADD up my bill, let's look in the ATLAS to find AFRICA, I like to go ANTIQUE shopping, this is very APPEALING, do you need AN ANSWER to your question? I APPRECIATE you; let us go AWAY together.... ANYWHERE you say. I AM running AFTER you. Look ABOVE up into the AIR! Whoops, did you have AN ACCIDENT, Is this AN ACTION hero? What ACTIVITIES shall we do today?

BE SURE that she can repeat some of these words back to you. Ask them if they can think of an "A" word? You will want them to think it through and respond. They will after a while as this becomes more familiar. If you comment using these words enough throughout the day, she will. Say the words you are focusing on while cooking dinner, dressing them, being in the car with any regular activity. Also comment when she uses an A word when she is speaking. Be very casual and matter of fact. Never say anything disciplinary or be negative in tone of voice or your actual words. This is not about minding. If they are not interested, just skip it for now. Drop the subject. But again it should all be so fun for them. Constantly reward them with attention and kisses from the teddy bear. When she is motivated, listening and getting it right, her curiosity and interest soar. But do not overdo this. If they are tired also drop this... Always leave them wanting more. Concentrate on one letter at a time for days, weeks, months...whatever it takes for success. There is certainly no deadline or hurry. But do try to be consistent.

PHUNNY "A" NAMES - AUGIE, ALDO, ABNER, AUNTIE EM, RAGGEDY ANN AND ANDY, ALADDIN

ANIMALS- ANTS, ANTELOPES, ALLIGATORS, ANTEATERS

FOODS- APPLES, APRICOTS, APPLESAUCE, AVOCADOS, ALMONDS, ALPHABET SOUP, ARROZ, APPLE PIE, ANIMAL CRACKERS, ARTICHOKES, ASPARAGUS

COLORS- AQUA

DOS

Be patient. TAKE YOUR TIME! Tell him how smart he is! Positive reinforcement is central to this program.

Knowing his ABCs will not teach him to read, but phonics (the noise that letters make) will. Put the noises together as you read their children's books...They are reading!!!

Smile and laugh with a very calm and casually fun demeanor.

Be in the moment and genuinely enjoy it. What a privilege to have a child!

Stop immediately when he loses interest, but FIVE minutes will be the perfect length of time for this along with a few comments throughout the day, but just here and there. .

DON'TS

Don't discipline him about this.

Don't force him to pay attention. Keep it very cool, casual, normal, and very fun.

Never speak down to your child

NOTE

These "noises" are the basic phonetic sounds. Some exceptions are included here, and may be easily learned and incorporated within this context. But it is the basic sounds that are important for now. After they have learned the basic sounds, then they can shift into the exceptions. You may be able to incorporate it within this framework saying yes ABLE, ANGEL, ACE start with the name of the letter. Sometimes this happens with other letters such as BEE, DELIGHT, GEE, I, OPEN, PECULIAR, TEA, ZEBRA. And yes, there are many more exceptions in the English language, but I found with my children that they easily shifted into the differences within the structure of this work. So please just start with the basic phonetic sounds that I am describing in these pages.

COME ON, LET'S PLAY LETTERS!!

B as in BAT

Draw a capital "B". It is a stick with two bumps or two half circles. See how it goes? The little boy "b" is a stick with just a little bump on the bottom. See how this looks? Can you see how it goes? Very good...wonderful. Tell your child that the name of the letter is B and the noise that it makes is ba baba

Can you say ba ba? Very good! Let me think of some B words. BABY...can you say BABY? Let me hear it again BABY with kisses and tickles from the teddy bear. BUBBLES IS A B WORD, BABY BEAR, BALL, BLOCKS, BARKING dogs, BIG kids, BIG BOYS, BUCKLE up BUTTERCUP! BELLY BUTTON, BEACH BALL, BANG, BOOM, BAM! Would you like a BUBBLE BATH? These are all B words. That makes the ba ba sound. Let's BLOW BUBBLES, Do you like BUGS? BIRTHDAYS? I am so glad that you were BORN, your sister is a BROWNIE, this is a BIG BED, BICYCLE, ohoh did you get a BOO BOO? Where is your BACKPACK? Where is your BANKIE? Shall we go to the BAKERY or the BOOKSTORE? BA BABA What a BEAUTIFUL BOUQUET of flowers. Want me to scratch your BACK? BOUNCING BALL, you are my BUDDY, Where is the dog's BONE? Can you see the BIRDIES/BIRDS in the sky? BOAT, let us look at the pictures in this BOOK, where is your BROTHER'S BASEBALL cap? Ring the BELL. This is a BIG fluffy BLANKET; choose the "B" words that fit into the moment. BOTTLES, BOX of cereal, where are your BOOTS? Where is your BRACELET? Look at that BIG BUS! This is a BABY BEAR. You are my BEST friend. ...my BEST BUDDY! This is BETTER than I thought. Where are the BEAN BAGS? What a BEAUTIFUL BOW for your hair. Take a BIG BREATH. Can you hear the BELLS ring? What shall we have for BREAKFAST? Please BRING me the BOX of crackers. Thank you. Let me BUTTON your sweater. Refer to this list often to bring up new words that demonstrate the "B" sound. Do you like BUNK BEDS? This is a BUMPY ride. Let's BAKE cookies. Let me BUCKLE your BELT. Let us go to your BEDROOM to find your BACKPACK. I love BARBECUES. BEES BUZZ around, and look so BUSY. I love to BRAID your hair, BOY am I hungry. Where is my BROOM? What a BEAUTIFUL BLUE sky today. What is going on in the BACKYARD? Where is your BATHROBE? Please sit in the BACKSEAT. BUCKLE up. This is a BRAND new BASKETBALL. Are you BAREFOOT? One more BITE please. BYE-BYE. What does the B say?

EXCELLENT! Tickle time. If she has forgotten, just keep explaining the sound. She will get it eventually. Be very patient. Now ask her what sound does the letter A makes? If she has forgotten and she probably has, go over it gently. This will all take a lot of repetition. Do not be concerned, or impatient with her progress. It takes as long as it takes for her to get it...

NAMES- BUBBA, BARNEY, BOO BOO, BUTCH, BUTTONS, BUBBLES, BUSTER, BUNNY

FOODS- BANANAS, BACON, BROCCOLI, BUTTER, BREAD, BAKED BEANS, BARBECUE, BURGERS, BLUEBERRIES, BANANA BREAD, BROWNIES

ANIMALS-BIRDS, BUNNIES, BUTTERFLIES, BULLS, BULLDOG, BUFFALOS, BEARS, BATS

COLORS: BLUE, BLACK, BEIGE, BROWN. What is the color of one of her stuffed animals?

Comment on the sounds of the first names of people in your family. By pointing out these sounds and all of the other sounds in the alphabet in your very positive and loving manner, you are also conveying love, subtle acknowledgment of their existence and their importance to you, this is the absolutely marvelous offshoot of this manner of teaching. She will really feel your love as you make the sounds come alive. Overcoming alienation between family members in our busy lives can be started early. Certainly surviving, earning a living, and making it through these hectic days take us away from the hearts of our children, but children need attention and a calm understanding of how much they mean to us. By pointing things out and listening to their responses will bring great fun and joy to both of your lives. Let them see how much fun they bring to your life, and how much they matter to you. Caring for very young children is not just custodial. Laugh with them and enjoy life together. It is great to be alive

More Dos

Be happy, relaxed and upbeat. If not, wait until you are.

Keep emphasizing that the name of the letter is different that the noise that it makes.

Keep repeating the noise that each letter makes over and over until she gets it...and then repeat it some more each day.

Remember that these learning opportunities with your child will strengthen your relationship with him. You now have something fun to talk about together that you both can enjoy. You will see....You will both love this learning experience.

I have many fun words as examples. You will have to choose the ones that elicit the best response. We want them to be amused, animated and excited about all of this, so you pick and choose which examples of the sounds are the best ones for you and her/him.

REMEMBER ONLY FIVE MINUTES OF THIS!!!

Yes, there are several sounds for each letter. The English language has many exceptions, but children are adaptable and seem to learn language quickly if you promote it. These words and methods are a great beginning, and are foundational for what they will later learn in school. They are now becoming familiar with the letters and the sounds. GREAT job on your part!! This is life changing for your babe!!

C as in CAT

Draw a capital C explaining that it looks like a circle with a part of it missing. It looks like a doggy took a big bite out of this circle, doesn't it? The little kid "c" is just like the big daddy "C" only smaller. The noise that the "C" makes is ca...ca...ca. Can you say that? Excellent! This is wonderful. I think that you may need a tickle...come over here. Chase him if need be.

Let me see what words start with the ca ca sound? I am thinking. Want a CUPCAKE while we watch CARTOONS? These are C words...ca ca... CANDLES on your birthday CAKE. Let me COMB your hair. I love these C words! CARS, COWBOYS, bats live in a CAVE. Let me COLLECT some COLORED pencils. A CABOOSE is the last CAR on a train. A CACTUS has stickies on it. Where is my CAMERA? CAN you do a CARTWHEEL? CONGRATULATIONS I think that you understand the C sound. Big tickle time. A few CR words for later, CRAYONS, CRACKLE, CRUNCHY, CROSSING, CRYING, CROWN, CRAWLING, CRUISING, CRUMBS, CRAFTS, CREATURES, CREATE, CRITTERS, CRYSTAL ball. A few CL word for later, CLOWN, CLOTHES, CLIMB, CLOUDS, CLAP your hand, let's CLEAN your room, that kitty has CLAWS! A few CH words for later, CHILDREN, CHIMNEY, CHEERFUL, CHILD, CHOOSE, CHEWY, CHRISTMAS, CHECKERS, CHALK. Let's CHAT

PHUNNY NAMES - CANDY, CRICKET, CHA CHA, COOKIE, CORKY, CURLY, CUTIE PIE.

ANIMALS- CATS, CAMEL, CATERPILLAR, COWS, COLT, CROWS, CHIPMUNKS, CROCODILES

FOODS-   CUPCAKES, CARROTS, COOKIES, HOT COCOA, CANTALOUPE, CAULIFLOWER, CORN TORTILLAS, CRACKERS, CHERRY PIE, CORN BREAD, ICE CREAM CONES, CRUST

COLORS- CREAM, CHOCOLATE

D as in DID

Draw a capital D saying here is a big stick "l" with a big bump on it or it has a half of a big circle on a stick. The little kid "d" is a stick 'l" with a little bump on the other side of the stick like this (as they watch you draw it.)

The name of the letter is D, and the D makes the noise of da dada. Repeat the sound of D. Say I am thinking of some D words. DING DONG, is that the DOORBELL? Hot DIGGITY DOG, DADDY. This is a beautifully DAY! You are my DARLING DAUGHTER, rub a DUB DUB...Where is your DUCKY? You are DAZZLING, let's go DOWNSTAIRS, let's go DIG in the garden, where is your DOLLHOUSE? Would you like a DRINK of water? Get DRESSED. Let's go for a DRIVE to get a DELICIOUS DINNER. Is it DARK outside? The sun has gone DOWN. This DESK is DUSTY, are your shoes DIRTY? Let's DOODLE...can you connect the DOTS? DIG DEEP in your pocket for some DIMES. What's for DESSERT? Have you DISAPPEARED? Are you DOWNSTAIRS? You are almost able to DRESS yourself. DO you feel DROWSY? DID you DREAM last night? What DAY is today? Where is my DICTIONARY? Let's DRAW. I love DAISIES, DAFFODILS. This is DELICIOUS and DELIGHTFUL Let's DO the DISHES. Let's play DOMINOES. DUNKIN DOUGHNUTS... DA DADA what else starts with the letter D? DUMP truck......do you hear the DA DA sound? Tickle time...Take it nice and slow...You are DOING fabulous DAHLING. Let's DANCE! This is DELIGHTFUL...Sweet DREAMS.

PHUNNY NAMES: DONALD DUCK, DAISY, DAFFY DUCK, DOODLES, DIMPLES, DUMBO, DISNEYLAND, DIXIE, DIZZY

ANIMALS: DOGS, DUCKS, DINOSAURS, DONKEY, DOLPHINS.

FOODS: DRUMSTICKS, DOUBLE DIP ice cream cones, cookie DOUGH, DILL pickles, DATE nut bread, DRESSING for your salad, DOUGHNUTS, DESSERT , DUMPLINGS, DRINK of water, DINNER

E as in RED

Draw a capital E and say here is a stick l with three little sticks going across it.....one, two, and three ...perfect. The little "e" is almost a circle with a little line in the middle.

The noise that this letter makes is eaea ea. Listen while I think of some E words...

Let me see.....hmmm we are ENJOYING ourselves with these words. How about EXCITING, EGGS, ELEPHANT, ELF. There are so many E words. Letters in the mailbox come in ENVELOPES. Let us do some EXERCISES. Where shall we EXPLORE today? Shall we take the ELEVATOR or the ESCALATOR? Is this the ENTRANCE? Can you say "ea" Marvelous!!!!...tickle time. What are some more E words? You are ENERGETIC and very ENTERTAINING. Are you ENJOYING EVERYTHING today? I am too. EXTRA scrambled EGGS for you? EXCELLENT....I love you EVERYDAY. You have cute EARS...the ENGINE in the car is here....do you want to see? Open up the hood to show him. I am EXPLODING with happiness. You are an EARLY bird this morning. Is your tummy EMPTY? Mine too. Let's EAT. An ENGINEER drives the train. Some ESKIMOS live in igloos. When is EASTER Sunday? You are very ENTHUSIASTIC! You did an EXCELLENT job! E sounding words.... EARRINGS, EASEL, EAT, EVEN, ELEVEN, EASY, EEL, ERASER, EARS......There are a number of exceptions with the "e" sound, but these will do for now. Remember to not rush or have too many expectations on how quickly this all will take hold. Just keep at it. It is amazing how easily they learn at this age. Never be in a hurry or seem upset or frustrated.

NAMES: ELMO, ELMER, AUNTIE EM. ELWOOD, EASTER BUNNY,

ANIMALS: ELEPHANTS, EAGLES, EELS, ELKS

FOODS: EGGS, ENCHILADAS, ENGLISH MUFFINS, EVAPORATED MILK, EGGPLANT

COLORS: EMERALD GREEN, EBONY

At some point you can start sounding out with your babe, the letters and words that appear every day whether on a cereal box, a magazine, a newspaper or the sign on the side of a passing truck. He will see and recognize some of the letters and the noise that they make. He won't get all of the letters, but this will be a great beginning and learning opportunity for further progress which is coming. Tell him that reading is just like putting together a jig saw puzzle. It is fun and it is so easy. Why not check out the comic pages in the Sunday paper. Sound out a few of the words. With every success, show him how happy and proud you are. Say " you are learning so quickly, what a smart boy/girl, I am so proud of you, you are amazing etc." The next day and remember that there is no rush. You can start on a new letter. Remember that just a few minutes a day are all that is needed. Don't let this become tedious or expect too much too soon. They know when you are frustrated or aggravated......NEVER let it get to this point. It is so fun and endearing to see them learn. They can do this.

Let's sound out the words...B-E-D, D-A-D, D-A-B, C-A-B? Tell her to put the sounds together...it's just like a puzzle. Ba-eh-da...Da ah da...Say it again and blend the sounds....Have her say the word...Be-eh-da....BED! DAD. She is reading!!!!! Tell her with great joy....YOU ARE READING!!! ...See how easy it is....Be

33

patient and do this blending slowly. When successful...many HUGS AND KISSES!!!

.Let's tell grandmother and your father.....YOU ARE READING.....Isn't this fun???? You are one smart kid!!! Let's try the word....CAB....Ca-ah-ba...again...Ca-ah-ba...CAB!!!YES!!!! This is so fun and so easy!!!

A-D-D....ah-da-da~~~~~ADD ...EXCELLENT

Now, don't hurry......take it easy.....There is plenty of time for this....and for success....Are you having a wonderful time? I hope so.

Children this age are darling and so loving. They get into mischief when they are not being stimulated, calmly challenged, or have things that are not interesting to them. They are just beginning to understand language and speaking, and this must be encouraged.

Very young children love to sit next to you and have your undivided, loving, and calm attention, and this is a great reason to do so. Wrap your arms around them. In a few years they will want to be running outside in more active pursuits, so now is the time. This is such a confidence builder and a fabulous background for their coming school years. Do not press hard or have a disciplinary attitude at all. Just teach one or two letter sounds at a time ....for a day or for a week. Stop just before they lose interest so that they look forward to the next time. And occasionally comment on words that you are teaching throughout the day in casual situations. Yes, there is a car.......ca caca car. That is a "C" word, isn't it? Very good. If he gets bored or distracted, stop immediately and drop the subject for a few days. There is no deadline for learning. Remember this is learning emphasized by a lot of fun. You can read the "Phunny

Stories" before they go to bed or anytime …Say use your imagination when I read them to you.,….Imagine them…They will love this, and the stories are funny…Ask her, "Which story is your favorite?".

Sesame Street is a great adjunct to this as they demonstrate words in a fun way with a phonetic emphasis. And there are other TV programs that do the same, but this is the work that will work and stick.

Are you noticing that your connection with your child is improving? While doing this, you will discover that you will have more in common and you will be enjoying each other's company. I loved this part.

F as in FUN

Here is a stick with two little sticks....can you see one little stick is on the top and one other little stick is in the middle. This is called "F." Can you say the name of the letter? Fabulous...tickle time. Now let's see the little kid f is a little stick with a little curve at the top and a very little stick through the middle. Now we know that the name of the letter is F, but the noise that it makes is fafafa. Can you say that? Fa, fa, fa FABULOUS. Now I am thinking of some words that start with the fafa sound. How about FATHER, FACE, FAMILY, FINGERS. FUZZY wuzzy was a bear, are you FUZZY? FOLLOW me... What else can I think of that starts with the letter F and says fafa? FIREWORKS on the FOURTH of July, FROGS in a pond. FISH have FINS. Please put the FORKS on the table. Thank you! You go FIRST. Your FRECKLES are adorable. Let's play FRISBEE. Let's make a FORT. Shall we read a FAIRY tale? What is your FAVORITE FOOD? Let's go to the FARMERS' market for FRESH FRUIT, FLOWERS and veggies. See the FIRE STATION. Let us have FOUR FABULOUS FRIENDS over FOR some FUN. Birds FLY in the sky, Your Dad loves FOOTBALL. Do we need FIREWOOD for the FIREPLACE? We need a FENCE, FE FI FO FUM. Do you see the FLAG FLYING high up on the FLAGPOLE? Let's go out to the FARM. You are my best FRIEND. We are having FUN today!! It is FREEZING cold in here. I need your FLUFFY blanket...FOLLOW me. Are your FINGERNAILS clean? You are a FAST learner. It is FIVE o'clock, and I need to FIX dinner. Are we FINISHED? FAREWELL

NAMES: FLUFFY, FROSTY, FOXY, FRECKLES

ANIMALS: FISH, FLAMINGO, FROGS, FLYING FISH

FOODS: FRESH FRUIT, FROSTING, FRENCH FRIES, FROZEN FOOD, FRENCH TOAST, FRITOS, FLAN, FRIED FISH, FLAPJACKS

COLORS: FIRE ENGINE RED

G as in GAS

A G looks just like a C but with a little table on it. See how it looks. The little kid g is a half circle with a little tail connected to it. This is a fun letter. The G makes the noise of gaga. Let me hear you say gaga ...perfect. When you see the G on a page you can say....gagaI know a bunch of words that start with the gaga sound. How about a GALLOPING horse, What GAME shall we play? Are you GIGGLING? GARAGE is where we put our car, let's do some GARDENING (plant mammoth sunflower seeds), GIDDY UP, let's GO, Are you acting GOOFY today? These are GOOD books! Let's GO outside to play. Do we need GAS for the car? Please close the GATE. A turkey GOBBLES, GOOD-BYE, GOD bless you. Is that a GOLD watch? You have GORGEOUS eyes, GOOD job! GUMDROPS, GUITAR, You are so GOOD looking! GO-GO cart, GOOD morning, GOOD night my sweetie pie, your Dad loves GOLF, This candy is GOOEY! Please GIVE me the GLASS please; Thank you for the beautiful GIFT, And into the GL sounds I am so GLAD that you are here, a GLASS of water for you?, where are my GLASSES? Where is your brother's baseball GLOVE? Where is the GLUE? GR words you look GREAT, GREAT to see you! You are a GREAT friend! You are GROWING fast, GREEN light means GO. GRANDMOTHER is coming, please play on the GRASS, Please sit in the GROUP, and let's not be GRUMPY today.

NAMES; GOOFY, GUMBO, GIGGLES, GINGER, GUMDROP, GUS, GOOGIE, GROVER. GRINCH

ANIMALS: GOLDFISH, GOPHER, GORILLA, GOOSE, GOAT, GIRAFFE, GRASSHOPPERS, GUPPIES

FOODS: GRAVY, GRAPEFRUIT, GARLIC BREAD, GRAPES, GRAHAM CRACKERS, GRAPE JUICE, GUM, GREEN BEANS, GROCERIES,

COLORS: GREEN, GRAY, GOLD

Now what words can she sound out now? How about BED, DAD, BAG, FED, BEG, ADD, EGG, BAD. Just say the sound of each letter, and then tell her to put the sounds together like putting a puzzle together....one sound moves into the next sound and you are reading the word!!!

Sound these out with great enthusiasm. She will get it...Be very patient and loving as you repeat over and over. This can take awhile, but she will get it, no matter how long it takes as long as you are not judgmental or impatient. Fully expect her to get it, and she will!!! This is called READING....!!! How about it, kids. I love it!!! And keep going.

Find a beautiful notebook and write out some three and four letter words. Check out my list at the end of this book. Have her sound them out slowly...When she gets them right...big hugs and kisses. Tell her that she is reading like the big kids do. Draw little stars next to the words she reads correctly. Think of a reward....stickers, a little bracelet, a little something. Throw in some big words that she loves too...flamingo and banana for instance. These are longer words that you will read later. Check out flamingo pictures on the Internet....gorgeous pictures of all descriptions esp. animals are at your fingertips, and they love to look at them with you. There are some pictures for coloring. Print out pictures of a few of the words she is learning to read.

Her world is expanding, and all under the umbrella of learning to read. I feel very strongly that this program will develop your child on many levels.

H as in HAT

A big daddy H has two sticks with a little monkey bar in the middle. That would be fun to swing on, wouldn't it? And the little boy "h" looks a little bit like a chair, doesn't it? The noise that the H makes a hae, hae, hae sound... Can you say hae? Excellent...perfect!! Let me think of the fun words with the hae sound...I know...HELLO, HOW are you? You are so HANDSOME! Want a HAMBURGER? (When you are in a hamburger place be sure to show him the word up on the sign) You are great at HELPING me today, HOORAY! Is it time for a HAIRCUT today? You have such beautiful HAIR! HALLOWEEN is in October. Let's play HOPSCOTCH. Can you do a HANDSTAND? Give me a HUGE HUG. This is HEAVEN! Shall we HUM? Are your HANDS clean? Let's draw a HAPPY face. HONK the HORN on your car. Where are the HANGERS? Where are you HIDING? This is HILARIOUS! Are you HAVING fun? Let's dig a HOLE in the garden. Bring the HOSE over HERE please. I will need a HAMMER for this. It is HOT outside today. Want to play a HARMONICA? Dad is my HUSBAND. We need to do some HOUSEWORK. I like to be at HOME. Let us draw HEARTS for Valentine's Day. Please HOP over HERE. I need a HUG!! HURRY please. Let's dance the HULA. Do you HAVE the HICCUPS? See the HELICOPTER? Are you HUNGRY? HO HOHO, the HOLIDAYS are coming. I love HOMEMADE cookies. HERE we go down the HALL. Let's play HIDE and go seek. I need another HUG!!!!

NAMES: HANSEL AND GRETEL, HONEY BEAR, HUMPTY DUMPTY, HOT LIPS, HUCKLEBERRY HOUND, HARRY POTTER

ANIMALS, HIPPOPOTAMUS, HORSE, HUMMINGBIRD

FOODS: HAMBURGERS, HONEY, HOT DOGS, HUEVOS RANCHEROS, HALIBUT

COLORS: HOT PINK

I as in IT

An "I" is just one long stick and the little girl "i" is just a little stick with a dot on the top.......see how this looks?

The noise that it makes is ieieieie.........can you say this? very good

Let me think of some words that begin with this sound........ IT'S a beautiful day, ITSEY bitsy spider went up the water spout, May I INTRODUCE my son, Lucas. Are you INVISIBLE? Very INTERESTING! You have a great IMAGINATION. Let's go INDOORS today; there is a lot of INFORMATION here. I need to check the INTERNET. Do I have enough INGREDIENTS for this cake? This IS IMPORTANT, IS this IMPOSSIBLE--no, What INNING IS this? Do you INSIST? Let me INSPECT this. This IS INSTANT fun, INCREDIBLE! INSECT bites make me ITCHY, INTO the woods we go, we need to INFLATE this ball, this IS one INCH....as you show him a ruler, You are IT. IGLOOS are where some Eskimos eat and sleep. Some of the American INDIANS live in Arizona. Let's INCLUDE the others. Let's INVITE some friends over for dinner. Let's play a musical INSTRUMENT. I am IMPRESSED with your learning these letters... Sometimes the letter I sounds the same as its name like .I love you, I love to read, I feel good, ICE cubes, I have an IDEA, IT IS ICY cold in the snow, I see ICICLES on the edge of the roof, Do we need ICING for this cake? There IS an ISLAND in the middle of the lake, want some ICE CREAM?

PHUNNY NAMES: IGGY, INKY, IGOR, IZZY, ICHABOD, INDIANA JONES,

ANIMALS: INCH WORM, IGUANA

FOOD: ICED HERB TEA, ICE CREAM, ITALIAN FOOD, ICING ON THE CAKE, ICY COLD

COLORS: ICE BLUE

J as in JUMP

A "J" looks like a big fish hook, doesn't it......see how I draw it? The little gut j is a small hook with a little dot on top see....beautiful... I love 'J" words ...who doesn't like JAM and JUMPING and JINGLE bells? Where is your JUMP rope? Can you see the JETS flying high up in the sky? Where are your JAMMIES? Let us get some JUICE. JUST for fun, let us try to JUGGLE. We have a couple of JOBS around here. Want to play on your JUNGLE gym? See you in a JIFFY. You run fast like a JACK rabbit... Your Dad loves JAZZ. JINGLE BELLS, JINGLE BELLS JINGLE all the way. What is this JUNK? I need to go to my JOB. Get the applesauce JAR, please. Are those JEWELS on her crown? Where is your JACKET? Let's JOIN the others. Where are your JEANS? Mr. JOHNSON is the JANITOR. JEEPER's creepers. I love a JACUZZI pool. JANUARY, JUNE AND JULY. Great JOB! What a great JOKE. You hit the JACKPOT. Let's go JOGGING. I get too much JUNK mail. Are you JUMPING for JOY? JOIN me, please. I feel JOYFUL! Want to JUMPROPE? You look adorable in your JUMPER. The JUKE box is JUMPIN'. Where are your JIGSAW puzzles?

NAMES: JINXIE, JASPER, JELLY BEAN, JUGHEAD, JOLLY ROGER, JACK IN THE BOX.

ANIMALS; JACK RABBIT, JELLY FISH, JAGUAR, JUNE BUG

FOODS: JUICE, JELLY, JAM, JERKY, JUICY FRUIT, JELLO, JELLY BEANS, CRACKER JACKS

How to Measure Success

1. Does she take an interest and have an awareness of letters that she sees around her whether in books or on signs while she is riding in the car? If not, then step up your energy and enthusiasm with this.
2. Does she try to say the sound of the letter than she is seeing now? Sometimes you have to encourage this.
3. Does she hear sounds and try to repeat them with great pride and happiness as she looks for your affirmations?
4. Does she try to sound out a word with the knowledge that she has now?
5. Does she say, Let's Play Letters and get excited about doing so?

It is hard to think of appropriate child friendly words. Refer to these pages often.

Watch videos on your computer with them.....Boys like Fire Trucks, Monster Trucks, Demolition of tall buildings, Volcanoes, Ships and Airplanes in storms...discuss what is going on. This is great for their awareness and vocabulary. Girls like Animals, and anything that is particularly interesting to them like Art, Crafts, Horses, Gymnastics, or any of the above. Find their interests. This could be very instructive for both of you.

Here are some more practice words...BLEND THE NOISES. It is just like putting a puzzle together.

KID, JACK, DID, HEAD, HAD. CAB

YOU ARE READING!!!!.....JUST LIKE THE BIG KIDS!!!!

K as in KISS

OK.....let us draw a "K." It has a stick with two lines, one goes up and one goes down like this like a slide. See how I am drawing it? Fantastic!! The little kid "k" does the same thing only smaller like this and you draw it...yes very nice

Now I am trying to think of K words. I love the word KISS, and how about KEYS, where are my KEYS? Please help me find my KEYS. Go KICK the ball. There are KIDS in the park. You are so KIND. Always show KINDNESS to others. You are a great KID. Did someone KNOCK on the door? Quit your KIDDING. Have you ever seen a KACHINA doll? Want to look in the KALEIDOSCOPE? Can you see through the KEYHOLE? Where are your KHAKI pants? Want to learn KARATE or KUNG Fu? See the guys in the KAYAKS? The dog is in the KENNEL. A KILT is a man's skirt in Scotland. A KIMONO is a lady's dress in Japan, KICK KICK those legs (when you two are swimming) who is in the KITCHEN? Let us fly a KITE. Let us KEEP your room neat. Want an airplane KIT? I am such a KLUTZ! Let's get the KINKS out of this. Are you the KING? KABANG, KEEP this in your pocket. OK? KABOOM.......did you fall down? Give me a big KISS. The dog eats KIBBLE. Where is the KITTY? Your brother goes to KINDERGARTEN. KER-PLOP, I just dropped my purse.

NAMES: KERMIT THE FROG, KING KONG, KOKO THE GORILLA, KIKI, KIRBY

ANIMALS: KITTENS, KOI FISH, KANGAROOS, KITTYS, A KID IS A BABY GOAT, KOMODO DRAGON

FOOD: KEY LIME PIE, KIWIS, KETCH-UP, KABOBS, KALE, KIDNEY BEANS FOR CHILI, KETTLE CORN, KAISER ROLLS,

COLORS: KHAKI

L as in LADY

L is another great letter. It looks like a stick with a little seat on it. L sounds like the first noise in the word LOOK.... I love it because LOVE starts with the letter, L...which is my favorite word... I LOVE you...Think about the letter can you feel your tongue curl up on the sides when you say the sound of the letter L? Let's us have some fun with the letter L. I am trying to think of some fun L words. LEGO starts with L. And how about LAP...sit on my LAP while we think of other L words.LEMONADE FOR LUNCH? I LOVE to hear you LAUGH; can you hear the L sound? LIPS, LADDER, LAKE I need to do LAUNDRY, I am so LATE, point to your LEG, I LOVE LEARNING new words, LIE down for awhile and rest your eyes, what a beautiful LEAF, I LEFT my LOTION in the other room, Want to play LEAPFROG? See you LATER alligator. LOOK at those strong LEGS; LET'S go play on the LAWN. Time to LEAVE or we will be LATE, This LOOKS LIKE a LONG LINE, I need my key to open this LOCK, I am a LUCKY LADY to have you for my son/daughter, Where is my LIST? The music is too LOUD, You are LEARNING beautifully, LISTEN to the LULLABY, Can you find the LEASH for the dog? Always LOOK both ways when crossing the street, LET"S LOOK up this word in the dictionary. I need my LIPSTICK, Can you reach the LIGHTSWITCH? LIGHTS out. LET'S LOOK at the pictures in this LITTLE book, I LOVE LICKING an ice cream cone, I will turn on the LIGHTS, LOTS of LOVE in this house, Shall I sing a LULLABY? I think that you need some LOTION, That would be LOVELY, Always develop a sense of wonder and joy in your child," You are so much fun, you make me LAUGH, I LOVE you."

NAMES: LOVEBUG, LULU, LUCKY, LAMBCHOP,

ANIMALS: LIONS, LAMBS, LADYBUGS, LIZARDS,

FOODS: LEMONS, LIMES, LETTUCE, LOBSTER,

COLORS: LAVENDER, LILAC

M as in MAT.

To write a big daddy M is to put two slides together like this. For the little kid m, put two little bumps together mmm. I can think of some MARVELOUS M words...MOTHER, MAMA. MOMMY, I love MUSIC, a cow says MOO, I love blueberry MUFFINS, MUFFY was MY little girl's big doll, the cat says MEOW...where are your MITTENS?, look at pictures in the MAGAZINE, MAILBOX? Can you see the MOUNTAINS? What a MESS! Let me see your MUSCLES, Wow... I have to go the MARKET for some MILK. What shall I MAKE for dinner? Point out words on signs and sound them out with your sweetie, Do you want a MOUSTACHE? This is MAGNIFICENT, Where is my MAGAZINE? How MANY MINUTES in an hour? MONSTER trucks. Is there a MOUSE in the MAILBOX? See yourself in the MIRROR? See the MOON? Good MORNING sweetheart, Let's play MARBLES, Want to play MAKE believe? Let's play some MUSIC! MOVE over, please...do you have MUDDY shoes? I am going to MEASURE how tall you are. I need a MAGIC wand, I believe in MIRACLES, Today is MONDAY, Halloween MASKS, This MUST be MAGIC, Please help ME MOP the floor, Where are the MUGS? Let's go to the MOVIES, I need to go to the MALL. Your shirt MATCHES your pants. You have wonderful MANNERS when you say thank you and please and excuse ME, You MELT my heart

NAMES; MUFFY, MIGHTY MOUSE, MICKEY MOUSE, MUFFIN, MAGIC, MINNIE MOUSE, MO, MUPPETS, MITTENS

ANIMALS: MOOSE, MONKEY, MOUSE, MICE

FOODS; MASHED POTATOES, MILK, MUFFINS, MARSHMALLOWS, MELONS, MEATBALLS, MEXICAN FOOD, MACARONI, MILKSHAKE

COLORS: MAROON

KEEP GOING...DON'T STOP NOW...YOU ARE HALF WAY THROUGH

Sound out every word that you see in their children's books or signs or in a restaurant or on TV....This becomes a moment of learning for your babe...Eventually she will start doing this on her own. It is a joy to see.

Learning the names and sounds of letters creates a lot of interaction between the two of you as you must be noticing. It is fun looking for words and letters in public places. It gives you two something to say to each other when you are out and when you are home. This is an added interaction that is a wonderful side benefit to this. They love the attention and time that you are devoting to them especially if you do this with love, a sense of humor, and admiration. This has to make both of you very happy. The bond between the two of you can only strengthen as long as you keep this light and happy. Don't overemphasize or demand any of this. Remember to make this all very casual, matter of fact, and loving. Are you seeing any progress? Review letters and sounds often. You will be surprised at how much they learn and remember. Be very patient and loving.

THESE FIVE MINUTES A DAY WILL CHANGE THEIR LIVES!!!!

"Education is like a magic door that opens to your dreams."

Malala, Nobel Prize winner

N as in NEST....

The big N is a slide with a stick in front of it....see how it goes. And the little n is like a little stick with a falling bump on it....Can you say the sound like it sounds in nest? NOODLES...do you like NOODLES? Have you ever seen a water NOODLE? Let me NIBBLE on your NICE little ear. Or maybe I will NUZZLE you...hmmmm... Can you see our NEIGHBORS? Is it NOON yet? NOPE? Do you know your NUMBERS? NO? NAME a couple...how about NINE, See my NEW dress! I love the flower called NASTURTIUMS, Your room is so NEAT...I love it, do you like my NECKLACE? Like Dad's NECKTIE? NEED a NEW shirt? Where are the NAILS? Letters make a NOISE, See the basketball NET? I NEED to read the NEWSPAPER, I have a NICKEL...NOBODY is home, Please put the NAPKINS on the table, I see your NOSE, I NEED to write a NOTE, NOTHING going on in here, What is your NAME? Let me look at your NAILS, NICE to meet you, this is NIFTY, It is NOISY outside. Let's make a NEST in your room where you can hide, It is a NEW day; I NEED to watch the NEWS. Where is my NOTEBOOK? You are so NICE! Where is my NECKLACE? Use your NOODLE I am going NEXT door NOW, Where is my NIGHTGOWN...NIGHT NIGHT... sleep tight

SILLY NAMES: NACHO, NEMO, NEWMAN, NORWELL, NICKLES, NIBBLES

ANIMALS...NANNY GOAT, NIGHTINGALE

FOODS: NECTARINES, NOODLES, NUTS, NACHOS, NUTMEG, NUT BREAD

COLORS: NAVY BLUE

O as in OX...

First let's draw and O....Draw a big circle for the big daddy O and a little circle for the little kid o...perfect....I am trying to think of words that start with the letter O...Let me think......hmmmmm.....Turn the light switch ON and OFF....Dad is at the OFFICE where he works, OH goody..OODLES of noodles, Please OPEN the door, Lets go OUTSIDE, Can you see the OCEAN? You look darling in that OUTFIT, Let's ORGANIZE your room, Look at the ORCHARD, Where are the Christmas ORNAMENTS? ON your mark, get ready ...go. What is in the OVEN? Shall we ORDER? What do you want? A pig says OINK, Look at the OPERA singer, let's give her a standing OVATION. You are OUTSTANDING,OH OH, OK, ONE step at a time, OH, yes, I will have more OATMEAL, Let's stay OVERNIGHT here, ORIGAMI is the Japanese art of folding paper, Granddad plays the ORGAN, He OOZES goodwill!. Let's have an OUTING, OUCH, Dinner in ON the table....Shall we eat OUTSIDE? OH my...OH my, Look at the OAK tree. It is ONE O'CLOCK, This is ODD. How OLD is this? How OLD are you? This is your ONLY OPPORTUNITY here, You are an ORIGINAL....ONLY you could be so sweet, You have OUTSMARTED me, You OOZE personality, We are all by OURSELVES, Let's go ONLINE, This is OUT of date, You are OUTRAGEOUS and OUTSTANDING, Put ON your OVERALLS, please, Can you roll OVER and OVER and OVER again, OH, do you have an OWIE? Where is my OVERCOAT? I am OVERJOYED with you!!!

NAMES: OZZIE, OTIS, OTTO, OSGOOD

ANIMALS, OTTERS, OWLS, OCTOPUS, OYSTERS, OSTRICHES, ORANGUTANS

FOODS: ORANGES, OREO COOKIES, OLIVE OIL, ONIONS, OLIVES, OATMEAL, ORANGE JUICE

COLORS: ORANGE, ORCHID, OFF WHITE,

P as in PAPA

PA PAPA It is a stick with a big bump at the top. The little p is a stick with a little bump just like the big P but it is moved down below the line.....Let me think of a couple of P words. PARK...let's go to the PARK, POP goes the weasel, PAPA, POOPSIE, what PAGE are we on?, PAPER, POTS and PANS, PAINTING, PUSHING and PULLING, PACK your backpack, PLEASE PASS the salt, Do you like PUPPETS? I like PUPPIES. Hi PUMPKIN. Want a PIGGYBACK ride? PERFECT, PEEK a boo, PROMISES, PIXIES, PENCILS, you have lots of PEP today, Dogs and cats have PAWS, lots of PEOPLE are here today, time for PRAYERS, where is my nail POLISH? You look cute in a PONYTAIL, What cha got in your POCKET? There are PILES of stuff in here, PATTY cake, PATTY cake... PRETEND that you are a doggy, let's PLAY ball, Are you a PIRATE, where is your PUZZLE? Do you like PAPER dolls? PENNIES, PICNICS, Let's have a PIECE of PIE? PITCH the ball, POPSICLES, POWDER PUFFS, I am so PROUD of you, you are my PAL!!!I love soft and PUFFY PILLOWS Want a PINATA for your birthday? PLEASE PICK up the PAPERS. PURPLE POLKA dots, PLAYHOUSE, PETALS on the flowers. I will always PROTECT you. A PUPPY is a PET. It is a POSTCARD from PENELOPE, Is there a PACKAGE at the door? No PEEKING, PING PONG is a great game, let's PAINT a PICTURE

NAMES: PETER PIPER, PETER PAN, MISS PIGGY, PADDINGTON BEAR, PORKY PIG. POOPSIE, POPEYE, POOKINS PEACHES, PETUNIA

FOODS: PANCAKES, POPCORN, PEAS, PIZZA, PEARS, PINEAPPLE, PUMPKIN PIE, POTATOES, PEANUT BUTTER, PEACHES, PLUMS, POLENTA,

COLORS: PURPLE, PINK, PASTELS

ANIMALS; POODLES, PARROTS, PUPPIES

Keep going...KEEP GOING! They are learning these sounds very well, and both of you are enjoying yourselves...KEEP UP THE GOOD WORK>>>IS THIS WORK? NO....keep putting the noises together to form a word. YES. They are reading!!!!

Ultimately, this program helps a child's view of the joy and incredible lightness of being in life within this framework of reading. Parent and child will have a more loving relationship as they explore his world together. A happy childhood fuels and creates a solid and secure adult life. I saw this with my children even though their father died in their teenage years.

Q as in QUEEN

qua qua...can you hear this sound? How can we draw this letter? Let me think...It is a circle with a little tail on it Q...very cute. Words that start with Q and has the quaqua sound are. QUICK, let's hide, QUIET, so they can't find us. Any QUESTIONS? If you ever have a QUESTION about anything, you can always come ask me...OK? The duck says QUACK QUACK. Aren't you snuggly under your QUILT on the bed??? QUIT your kidding, I feel a little QUEASY, let's save QUARTERS and put them in your piggy bank, this is QUIRKY, We need a QUART of milk, I need Q-tips, don't QUIT now, Here is a QUIZ...what time is it? See the QUARTERBACK on the football team, a QUARTET is four people singing, I am QUIVERING over here, this is QUITE delicious, May I QUOTE you? I am the QUEEN!

NAMES; QUINCY, Q, QUEENIE, Q TIP

ANIMALS; QUAIL

FOODS; QUICHE, QUESADILLAS, QUAKER OATS

ALMOST DONE!!

R as in RUN.

How can we draw this letter? Looks like a stick with a bump and top and a slide in the middle....see how it goes. The little guy r is a little stick with a little on it....very cute...Now I am trying to think of R words...ROCKING horse and ROCKS outside...READING books. You are READING now!!!! Where is your RUBBER ducky? Let's go to a RESTAURANT. See any animals on the ROOF? The bark on the tree is ROUGH. Is that a RED light? Do you REMEMBER what the R says?? Let's go for a RIDE... Is it RAINING outside? Get your RAINCOAT and let's go outside to look for RAINBOWS ...ROW ROWROW your boat, Where are your ROLLER skates? Where is your RACING car? Let's go outside and smell the ROSES. Where is my RECIPE book? I think that I need to REST. Let's RELAX for awhile. Want to RACE? We need to RAKE the leaves, Do you like my RINGS? READY, get set go...You are REMARKABLE. Let's READ a story, REPEAT after me. I need RIBBONS for this birthday present, Can you see the RIVER from here? Swing from the ROPE, See the ROAD in front of our house, you are so RIGHT, Where is my ROBE? You are an excellent RUNNER, Let's listen to music on the RADIO. Can you REACH the RED book? We need to REPAIR this; do you need to be RESCUED? You need a REWARD, Do you like RAINY days? I do. Let's clean up your ROOM, ROUND and ROUND we go, I love READING to you. Are you ROLLING around on the floor?

NAMES: RUSTY, RUBY, ROCKY, RED, ROSIE, RIP VAN WINKLE, RUSTY

ANIMALS; REINDEERS, RABBITS, ROOSTERS, ROADRUNNERS, RACCOONS, RHINOCEROS

FOODS, RAISINS, ROAST BEEF, RASPBERRIES, RIBS, RICE, RICE CRISPIES, RADISHES

COLORS; RED, RUST, RASPBERRY

S as in SAT

This is a fun letter to draw .Draw a little wiggly snake for the capital letter, S, and an even smaller little wiggly snake for the little guy "s." Perfect.....There are so many great S words. You are my SON, SHE is your SISTER, and you are SO SILLY, Let's SING a SONG. Where is the SOAP? I love SATURDAYS, Let's go to SUNDAY SCHOOL, SUPERMAN, Where are your SOCKS? Want to SING in the rain? Let's go to the SUPERMARKET because I need SOME SOUP, want a SANDWICH? I love the SAND at the beach, Where are your SANDALS and SUNGLASSES? It is SUMMER! Want to go SURFING? Where is your bathing SUIT? Can you SEE the SAILBOATS? The SUNSHINE is out today; let's find the SEE-SAW. Can you hear the bacon SIZZLE in the pan? You are the SUNSHINE of my life, Oh, you SURPRISED me! We have SECONDS before we have to leave for SCHOOL, You love your SANDBOX. You are SAFE here. You are always SAFE with me. Want to play SOCCER or SOFTBALL? Put on your SEAT BELT, please. Let's SURPRISE Daddy! Please SET the table, SATIN feels SO SMOOTH! SOUND out the SOUNDS of the letters. Can you read the SIGNS on the trucks? SP sounds: You are SPLASHING in the water. You need a SPOON. Rockets go up into SPACE. You are SPEEDY today. This is SPOOKY. You have a lot of SPUNK! Your eyes SPARKLE! It is SPRINKLING outside. This is SPECTACULAR! SW sounds...SWEET dreams SWEETHEART, You are my SWEETIE pie. Let's go SWIMMING. Want to SWITCH sides? Where is your SWEATER? SL sounds... Are you SLEEPY? I think that it is STORYTIME! I like the SLIDE at the park. See the SLEEVE on your coat. Where are your SLIPPERS? The cement is SLIPPERY.

Are you SLURPING? I love your SLINKY SK sounds...Let's SKIP rope. Can you SKIP along the sidewalk? The kids are SKATING today on roller SKATES. You have soft SKIN. Look at the SKY today. SN sounds. Did you SNEEZE? Is that a SNOWMAN? Where is your SNORKEL? Are your SNEAKERS under the bed? Is it SNOWING? SNOOPER is a cute dog name. Are you SNUG as a bug in a rug? SC sounds. Where are my SCISSORS? One SCOOP or two? Do you like your SCOOTER? Let me SCRATCH your back... Let's go to SCHOOL. SH sounds...See your SHADOW? I like your SHOES. Let's STAY in the SHADE. Where is your SHAMPOO? SEE any SHOOTING STARS? What SHAPE is this? Please SHARE. See the SHIP, We need to go SHOPPING. Where is the SHOVEL? Time for a SHOWER. Please SHUT the door, please....SM sounds. You have the most beautiful SMILE. Do I hear the SMOKE alarm? This is lip SMACKING good! ...ST sounds. Where are the STAMPS for this letter? Let's go outside to look at the STARS. This is your STOMACH. STOP before you cross the STREET. The baby is riding in the STROLLER Oh boy, there is a STORM coming. I need to go to the STORE. You are so STRONG! SQ Please SQUEEZE the toothpaste, Where is your SQUIRTGUN? The blocks are SQUARE. The pillow is SQUISHY. Are you SQUAWKING?

SP You are SO SPECIAL to me!!!!

NAMES: SANTA CLAUS, SKEETER, SUPERMAN, SESAME STREET, SKIPPY, SYLVESTER, SPEEDY, DR. SEUSS, SPARKY, SPANKY, SNIFFLES, SHORTY, SUGAR, SWEET PEA,

ANIMALS: SEALS, SNAILS, SQUIRRELS, SPIDERS, SNAKES, STARFISH, SWANS, SKUNKS, SEAGULLS

FOOD: STRAWBERRIES, SOUP, SANDWICHES, SALADS, SPAGHETTI, STEAK, SNACKS, SNOW CONES, SUNFLOWER SEEDS, SALSA, SALT

T as in TOP....

What does the T look like? Let's see... Here is a little stick with a little table on top...This is the big T. The little girl t is a little stick with another little tiny stick through the top of it...see how this looks....I am thinking of some great "T" words...hmmm. How about TICKLE, TRICYCLE, TOYS, TRICK or TREAT....can you hear the ta tata sound...excellent ...TOOT your whistle, TABLE, TOOTHBRUSH, TAIL,TOAST, you are TALENTED, TASTES good to me, TAP dancing, This is TEENY TINY...TARGET, TREE, TEETER TOTTER, TELEPHONE, TELEVISION, TERRIFIC, TIRES on the car, Can you stand on your TIPPY TOES? Where is your TOWEL? Where is your TEDDY Bear? Let me TUCK you in. Let's go on a TRIP. THANK you, where is your daddy's TIE, your sister, TRACY is a TEENAGER, let's get a TENT, TWINKLE TWINKLE little star, TEN and TWO are TWELVE, are you TEASING me?, I hear THUNDER, I love to play TENNIS, We live in a small TOWN, lots of TRAFFIC TODAY, See THE TRACTOR and THE TRAIN? , please TAKE the TRASH out, THANK you for always TELLING me THE TRUTH, You will never be in TROUBLE for TELLING me THE TRUTH, We have to TRUST each other, Is your hair TANGLED?. Want to TUMBLE? We need TREATS for the dog, Where are your TENNIS shoes, TRUCK, TUG o war, TULIPS, I'll TRADE ya., THIS TASTES great, They are TWINS, Let's play TAG, Please TAKE TURNS, She is a TODDLER. TIME to eat, TIME to go see Grandmother, TWIST and TURN, THANKS a lot, TOODLE LOO, TIME to TUCK you in bed

NAMES: TWEETY PIE, TAFFY, TANGO, THUMPER, TINKERBELLE, TOOTSIE

FOODS: TUNA SANDWICHES, TACOS, TOMATOES, TURKEY, TOAST, TORTILLAS, TOMATO SOUP

ANIMALS; TIGERS, TURKEYS, TURTLES,

COLORS: TURQUOISE, TAN

U as in UP.

The big U looks like a roller coaster. Move your hand and arm in the air to make a noise as you show her the swooping form of a U. The little kid "u" is just a little roller coaster. Now let me think of words that start with the letter U...UP we go, UP in the sky, This is UTTERLY delicious, Are you UNDER the bed, Where are your UNDIES?, UGH! Please don't put your feet on the UPHOLSTERY. Thank you, Where is the UMPIRE, You are so UNIQUE, Let us UNITE! We live in the United States of America, Let us UNROLL this paper, you have UNLIMITED talents, Want to UNWRAP your presents? This is UNUSUAL!, Can you push your bike UPHILL? Let me see your UPPER teeth, I feel UPBEAT today, do you feel UNSTEADY on your bike? You will be fine, Are you UPSIDE down? Please go UPSTAIRS, I am URGING you to listen, This is URGENT, Are you UNCERTAIN?, You are the sweetest kid in the whole UNIVERSE!, Are you in the UTILITY room?, I used to play a UKULELE, The gopher lives UNDERGROUND, This is the ULTIMATE, UGG! You are UTTERLY wonderful, this is ULTRA light, where is my UMBRELLA? I UNDERSTAND Let me UNDERLINE that, Let's go UNDER water, These lines are UNEVEN, Don't be UNHAPPY, I need to make a U-Turn, You are UNFORGETTABLE, Where is your UNIFORM?, Let's UNFOLD your clothes, This is UNFAMILIAR, Let me UNTIE your shoelace, This is UNTHINKABLE, Let's UNWIND the fishing line, Are you UPSET?, This is UTTERLY delicious. Let me UNDO your buttons, You have my UNDYING devotion. Don't be UPSET, let US UNWRAP the package,

NAMES: Uncle Sam, URCLE, UBBIE

ANIMALS: UNICORN

FOODS: UPSIDE down cake

V as in loVe.....

This letter looks like two slides that come together at the bottom. VA VA VA...Let's see, what word starts with the letter V? Hmmm How about a VALENTINE, yes, on Valentine's Day...Let's VISIT the library. I need to VACUUM this place. VILLAGE, VELVET material, a bride's VEIL, Isn't this a great VIEW? Monkeys swing on a VINE, VERY good, you are so VALUABLE to me, Phoenix is in the VALLEY of the Sun, I VOTED today, we need to VACATE this place. Is that a VIDEO game? She lives in VIRGINIA. See the VINES on the wall? Let's VISIT grandmother, you have a beautiful singing VOICE, See the picture of the VOLCANO? There is a big VOLCANO in Hawaii. We need a VACATION, Dad needs to take the dog to the VET, I love VELVET. I VOTE for that. Where is a VASE for these flowers?, You look so handsome in your VEST!, Want to play VOLLEYBALL?, Hear the VIOLINS?, See the moving VAN?, VA VAVA VOOM, We need a new VIDEO player, VISIT with me, Teach your child VIRTUE and he will be happy and free forever...You know VIRTUE....aligning your life, actions, and thoughts to ethical and moral principles. Any VAMPIRES around here? Did you VANISH? I can see the VEINS in your hand, You are VERY wonderful. This is a VENDING machine, VENUS is a plant. I need a VACATION. Did you VANISH? You are so VALUABLE to me. They need VALET parking here. I need the VACUUM cleaner. I feel like a VAGABOND today. There is a VARIETY of activity here. You won a VICTORY, I need my VITAMINS

NAMES: VENUS, VITO, VLADIMIR,

COLORS: VIOLET

FOOD: VEGETABLES, VANILLA ICE CREAM, VEGGIE BURGERS, VEGETABLE SOUP, VINEGAR

If you need to calm them down, try 2 cups of apple cider vinegar in a bath...Let them play for 20 mins...worked miracles for me...

W as in WOODS....

I want to draw two Vs stuck together like this....Yes! The little kid w is two little "v"s stuck together....How about that? Now I am wondering about the W sound and the words that start with this sound...wawawa...WOW, WAKE-UP angel! WIGGLE and giggle, the dog says WOOF WOOF and WAGS his tail, Let's WATCH the WAVES at the beach and the WATER skiers, Let's WAIT here. WANT some WATERMELON? Are you WARM? Please finish this WORK, I am WISHING for some WAFFLES! WATCH me. I love WORDS. You are WELCOME, It snows in the WINTER, See the WATERFALL? The dog is WET! WHERE are you? Can you see out of the WINDOW? This is WINTER. Make a WISH. WHOOPS! Beautiful WEATHER, Dad is in the garage WORKING at his WORKBENCH, Tomorrow is WEDNESDAY, The kitty has WHISKERS, WE are going to a WEDDING. I am a WOMAN. WHERE is your WAGON? WHISTLE, WHAT? WHEN? WHY? WHERE? WHOOPSIE. This is the WALL. Let's go for a WALK. We need to WASH the dishes. He is always WELCOME! Please WATCH me. I need to WAX the car. WAVE goodbye. What do you WANT to WEAR today? You are so WELL-behaved. That is a WHEELBARROW. WAY to go! a duck WADDLES, the earth is also called the WORLD. That is the WHITE House where the President lives. You are WONDERFUL. You are learning a lot of WORDS. Let's WRAP this present. WOW! WIGGLE on over here.

NAMES; WINNIE THE POOH, WIZARD OF OZ, WOODY, WALDO, WHOOPIE, WIGGLES

ANIMALS: WOLVES, WOODPECKERS, WORMS, WHALES, WILD ANIMALS, WALRUS.

FOODS: WAFFLES, WALNUTS, WHEAT, WHOLE WHEAT BREAD, WATERMELON. CHICKEN WINGS,

COLORS: WHITE

X as in boX....

The big X looks like two sticks crossing each other....Can you do that with your fingers? The little kid x are two little sticks crossing together.... Excellent....Words that start with the X sound...Let me think. There are not very many words that start with the letter X....How about X-RAY, XMAS, XEROX and XYLOPHONE

Y as in YELLOW.

Here is a popsicle stick with a V on the top for a big daddy Y...The little kid y is a little v with a little slide on the bottom that goes this way under the line...see how this goes? I am now thinking of some Y words ...YES, YUM YUM, This frozen YOGURT is so YUMMY! I love YOU!!! Are YOU three YEARS old? YES? YOU are YOUNG! That is a YORKSHIRE TERRIER. I love New YORK. Are you ready YET? YAKITY YAK, don't look back...Are we there YET? Where is my YO-YO? Do you have YOUR YO-YO? I need to YAWN! YIKES, it is time for my YOGA, YES? YOU are a YOUNGSTER, the dog is in the YARD, Please don't YELL, YOU are very special to me, Where is my YARN? YEP I see it, please help YOURSELF to some more YAMS. What YEAR is this? YAHOO! YABBA dabba doo! What YEAR is this? Where is your YELLOW jacket? I love YOUNG people .What happened YESTERDAY? YOU are wonderful! Did he YANK that away from you? Are YOU YOWLING? Can you YODEL? YIPPEE! YES, please. YOO hoo, I am over here. Be YOURSELF.

NAMES: YOGI BEAR, YODA, YANKEE DOODLE

ANIMALS: YAKS

FOODS: YAMS, FROZEN YOGURT, YELLOW SQUASH, EGG YOLKS

COLORS: YELLOW

Z as in ZOO.

Here is one line up here and one line down here with a little slide between them. See how that looks? I love the sound of ZZZZ. Let me sound out the sound with you....Let's go to the ZOO, ZIG-ZAG, Is your ZIPPER stuck?, ZAP, ZERO is a big round 0, ZING, What is our ZIP CODE, ZIPPITY DOO DAH ZIPPITY YEA, my oh my what a wonderful day...You are ZOOMING, ZAINY Brainy, ZONE, ZOWIE, Let's ZIP along? A ZITHER is a musical instrument, Are you a ZOMBIE today? ZING, ZIPPO, it is over. This is ZANY. My ZINNIAS look beautiful. You are so full of ZEST! Let's get this done ZIPPIDY quick.

ANIMALS: ZEBRAS AT THE ZOO

FOODS: ZUCCHINI squash, ZABAGLIONE, ZUPPA,

NAMES: ZOOMER, ZEKE, ZORRO, ZIPPO, ZIGGY

Now we get to the good part...the exciting part...Knowing most of the sounds is not enough. NOW is the time to really focus on blending the noises together to actually read a word. Sitting with her on the couch is the way to go ...one on one as you hold and reassure her in a loving tone of voice. Teaching your child how to blend the sounds is the next very important step to reading. She has graduated to this point, and you cannot let this moment slip by. The sounds are in her and now is the time to put them to positive use. Most DVDs stop before accomplishing this very important next step. Write some two and three letter words taken from the lists here on a cute notebook...great paper or a chalk board and carefully sound

75

them out with her. Take your time being very calm, patient and loving. Don't forget FIVE minutes!!! Laugh if you can...Always use the words that have special and fun meaning to her, CAT, DOG,..you know the right word to use. Then when she gets it right, give her tons of hugs and kisses,...That is wonderful...You got it...Do you know that you are reading..STARS for you and maybe a little present or treat. "This is fabulous. I think that I will give you a star for every word you read!!"...Be loving and enthusiastic. She will be so happy. Remember that their attention span is limited, but reading with her will amaze you and her. The best five minutes that you can send with her!!!

START WITH THE WORDS BELOW...

THREE LETTER WORDS TO SOUND OUT

ANT	CAT	HAT	JET
RED	PAT	BAM	SAT
BAG	SAT	RAT	CAR
BED	BAT	GAS	FAR
POT	DIG	JAR	NUT
BIG	JAM	HIM	PIG
CAN	DAD	BIG	NAP
PAN	TOP	FAR	OUT
DOG	WIG	MAP	PET
CAP	BED	MAP	HOP
HOT	MOP	GET	PUP
POT	POP	BUT	PUT
HUM	CUP	MOP	RAG
BAD	BUS	BAM	SUN
CAR	YUM	BOO	YES
FAR	EAT	ASK	TOP
JAR	MOM	BEE	ZOO
SAD	DAD	DIG	BIG
TOY	END	AND	TAG
BAG	CUP	MUG	MAD
PIG	HIT	SIT	BOO

FOUR LETTER WORDS

PARK	LONG	HELP	KISS
BIRD	HOOP	MIND	LEGO
WORD	GOOD	MELT	SOFT
FROG	LOCK	NECK	LAMP
HAND	SOAP	TICK	TOCK
BALL	KITE	BUZZ	KING
GOOD	TALK	HOME	BUGS
BOOK	BOAT	BEAR	ROCK
KICK	YARD	PAIL	HOOK
READ	KIDS	LOUD	BOYS
CALL	BALL	BATH	KIND
STOP	HILL	ANTS	BUMP
COAT	COLD	DOLL	FLAG
EGGS	FORK	FORT	FISH
FLIP	SWIM	DOGS	HARD
GIRL	SAND	HAND	SEND
WALL	FILL	TOLD	SIDE
COLT	THIS	SELF	MELT
BELT	FEEL	BELL	SOUP
HIDE	SEEK	DUCK	BEAK
FOLD	STEP	SEAT	GATE

Have her memorize the little common words: THE, IN, ON, AND, A, IS, THEY, etc.

HAVE HER READ THESE PHRASES AND LAUGH

Put the duck in the truck   The car is red.

Hop over the mop.   Ten pens

The baby blows bubbles.   Monkeys in rockets

The fish is in the dish.   Birds in a jar

Ten turtles under a tree.   Pig in a blanket

Egg in your ear.   Cat in a Hat

Spoon on the moon...   Baby Bugs

Pink ink   Pink Sink

Fuzzy wuzzy was a bear.   Dig Deep

Rocks in your socks.   Bug on the wall

Mouse in the house.   Hug me

Pig on a pillow.   Silly Billy

Boo Hoo.   Silly Goose

Mouse in your socks   Let's go

Nose on your pillow   Jump Up

Egg on your nose   Pup in the mud

The next step in keeping this process moving along beautifully is to keep going over the sounds here and there in everyday conversation. Have them read out loud the simple stories in their books. Keep the praise and admiration going strong. YOU ARE READING!!! They have learned the basic sounds, and to keep them motivated, remind them of these as you go along in life. As you are out driving, the words on buses or signs at stores or restaurants letters, words and sounds can be pointed out. Words are everywhere...use them for this purpose.

Your children have a fabulous start now. You have all of the tools from start to finish for them to read before attending school or for them to at the least know many of the sounds that will catapult them into a successful experience in kindergarten and grade school. Even if they just learn a few letters they still will have a big advantage, but expect more from this process. It is really very amazing. And again their teachers will be blown away by their ability which translates into premium attention from them, and your child's self-esteem will soar. HAVE FUN WITH THIS!!!!

SPECIAL GIFTS FOR READERS

If you are ready to improve your child's life even further, you will find more great resources at our website

www.childrensreadingsuccess.com.

Let's see how together we can kick start your child's journey to an amazing life.

Best,

Louise Moore

ABOUT THE AUTHOR

Louise V. Moore, a graduate with a B.A. in English from the University of Southern California, a high school English teacher, and a lover of poetry and the written word, has created a book about early childhood reading education. Some have called her the Mrs. Doubtfire of reading with her knowledge and storytelling ability. She has a book coming out soon with alphabet stories that will be a delightful companion book to Preschool Reading Success.

Her granddaughter is now the best reader in her first grade class who can read 120 words per minute with 100% comprehension along with her own now grown two children who also excelled with reading. All were taught using the methods in this book.

This book is dedicated to all children who will be given an extraordinary chance to excel at an early age. This will change their whole outlook on going to school, and bring confidence and encouragement about what it means to be educated. Ultimately, it is my mission to not only teach early childhood reading, but to emphasize to parents and caregivers to surround their children's learning on all subjects with a loving, exciting, stress free, and fun environment.

www.childrensreadingsuccess.com.

CPSIA information can be obtained
at www.ICGtesting.com
Printed in the USA
LVHW111113171222
735432LV00018B/277

9 781514 347935